Introduction

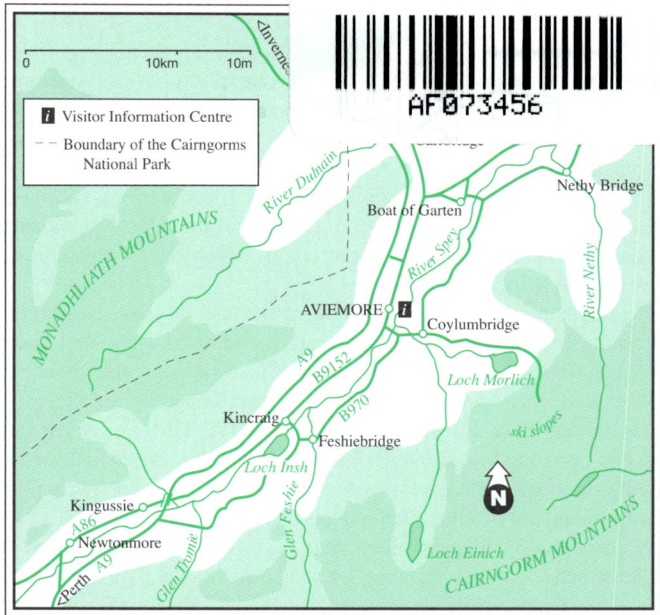

The area covered by this book (which lies largely within the boundary of the Cairngorms National Park – *see* map) comprises that portion of Strathspey – about 20 miles in length – between Newtonmore in the south and Grantown-on-Spey in the north, plus the hills to east and west. To the west of the valley are the Monadhliath Mountains (*Walks 5,21,22*): low, rolling, moorland hills; somewhat featureless and undramatic by the high standards of Scottish hill scenery, but with a quiet charm of their own. To the east of the valley are the Cairngorms: the greatest concentration of high peaks in Scotland, and justly recognised as one of the very best areas for walking in the country (*10,11,12,14*). The range is comprised of high (3500-4000ft) plateaux and rounded ridges eaten into by cliff-edged corries and steep, narrow glens. The hills undoubtedly carry dangers

– cool summit temperatures and swiftly changing weather conditions take their toll annually – but a clear, calm day amongst the Cairngorm peaks is an experience not to be forgotten.

On the north-western slopes of the mountains are the Cairngorm ski slopes (*11*), and the road running up to these slopes from Aviemore passes through a broad, wooded glen, flanked to the north by the ridge of Meall a' Bhuachaille and its neighbours (*4,6*). At the centre of this glen is little Loch Morlich (*7,12*), surrounded by conifer woodland. Much of the forestry in the glen is commercial, but there are also large areas of self-seeded pine forest: the remnants of the type of woodland – Scots pine, juniper and intermixed broad-leaved trees – which once covered much of the Highlands.

Rothiemurchus Forest, to the south of the road, is criss-crossed by footpaths running through the woodland and moorland, and past Loch an Eilein (*8,9,13,14*). To the west of the Cairngorms are the lower hills of Badenoch, through which run the narrow, parallel valleys of Glen Feshie (*16,17,20*) and Glen Tromie (*15,19*). Glen Feshie carries one end of a long footpath to Braemar and Glen Tilt, while paths from Glen Tromie lead over to Blair Atholl and Glen Garry. Such long tracks should not be attempted without suitable preparation.

Between these hills and moors runs the broad valley of the Spey, with its lochs, marshes, farms and woods (predominantly birch and pine). There are numerous small villages and hamlets in the valley, plus the three main towns of (from the south) Newtonmore (*21,22*), Kingussie (*18,21*) and the tourist centre of Aviemore (*5,24*). Much of this area can be explored on the Badenoch Way (*15*), which runs from south of Aviemore to Kingussie.

In addition, there are the smaller centres of Carrbridge (*5,23*), Dulnain Bridge and Nethy Bridge (*2,3*) where the valley widens out to the north of the highest hills, plus the sizeable town of Grantown-on-Spey (*2*).

Carnachuin Bridge, upper Glen Feshie (Walk 17)

1 Loch Garten_____C

Three signposted forest walks, two leading past small lochs. Part of a nature reserve noted for its nesting ospreys. Length: **all routes approximately 2 miles/3km**; *Height Climbed:* negligible. *O.S. Sheet 36*

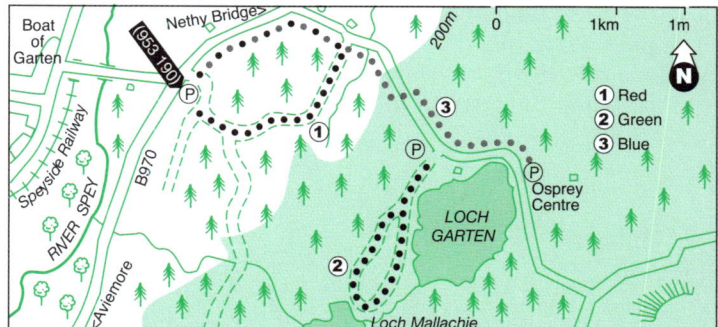

The return of the osprey to Scotland in significant numbers has been one of the great success stories of wildlife management. Loch Garten holds an honourable place in this story since it was here, in 1959, that a pair nested in Scotland for the first time since the early 20th century. The osprey is now likely to be seen by observant walkers throughout the central Highlands. For those who wish to be more certain of their quarry, however, a pair of the birds can still be seen each year at the Loch Garten nest site between late April and the end of August. The area is maintained as an RSPB nature reserve, and a visit can be combined with a walk along the signposted trails through the pine woodland adjacent to the loch.

To reach Loch Garten, drive north from Aviemore on the B9152, then continue along the A95 road for Grantown-on-Spey. Five miles north of Aviemore, turn right onto the minor road for Boat of Garten. Drive through the village, across the River Spey, and on up to the junction with the B970. Turn left along this. After a very short distance there is a car park to the right of the road, giving access to the walks.

This is the quietest of the three car parks, but it is at the opposite end of the routes from Loch Garten. To start nearer the loch, continue along the B970 for a short distance, then turn first right up a minor road, signposted for the loch. The first car park is about a mile along this road; the Osprey Centre car park half a mile further on.

There are three signposted walks through the pine woods: Red, Green and Blue routes. The Blue route is a lineal path linking the car parks.

2 Nethy Bridge & Grantown — B/C

A) *Six waymarked, predominantly woodland walks around Nethy Bridge.*
Length: from **1½ miles/2.5km** *to* **3½ miles/5.5km**. **B)** *A longer, predominantly woodland path linking Nethy Bridge and Grantown-on-Spey. Length:* **8½ miles/14km (one way)**; *Height Climbed: undulating.*
C) *Six waymarked walks through the woodland of Revack Estate. Length:* **½ mile/1km** *to* **5 miles/8km**.

O.S. Sheet 36

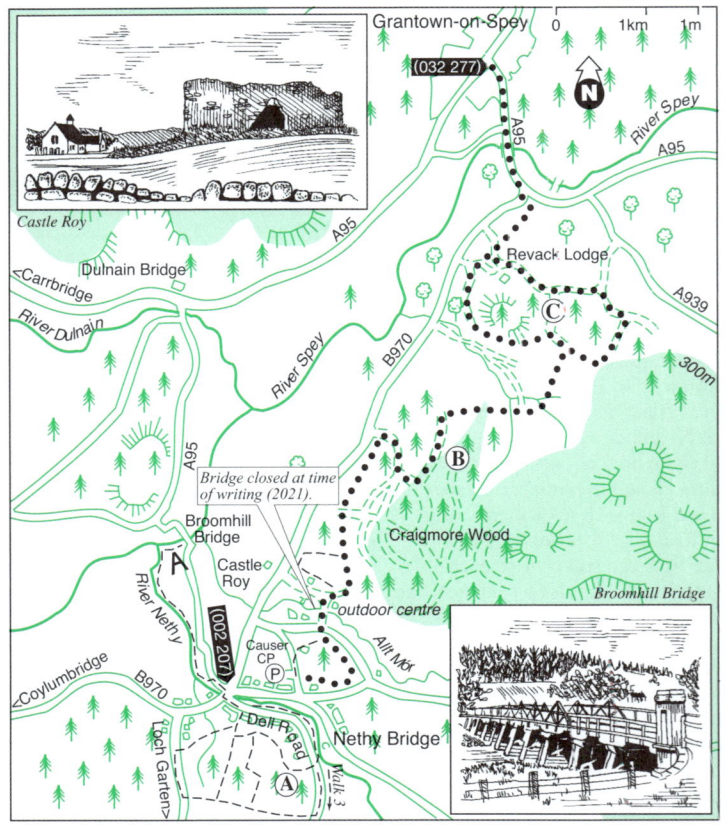

Grantown-on-Spey originated as a planned village, built in the late 18th century by Sir James Grant. It grew in the 19th century when it became a popular holiday resort, and it remains popular to this day – particularly with those interested in salmon fishing in the nearby River Spey.

Three miles upstream the Spey is joined from the south by a tributary: the River Nethy. One mile up the Nethy from the junction is Nethy Bridge: a pleasant little village with a golf course and a large hotel.

In the 18th and 19th centuries the district of Abernethy exported large quantities of timber, which was floated down the Nethy and the Spey to the coast, and was subsequently used for construction, naval supplies, railway sleepers, etc.

Walk A) The shallow slopes around Nethy Bridge are still clothed with pine forest – now largely managed for conservation purposes. A series of short, colour-coded walks have been laid out through the trees, providing a painless introduction to the flora and fauna of the native highland pine forest. In addition, another route – The Broomhill Walk (red) – follows the River Nethy down to its junction with the Spey, and to the wooden Broomhill Bridge which carries a minor road across the larger river (*see* map).

A map showing the routes of the walks is shown on the information board a short way up Dell Road from the village shop.

Walk B) One of the signposted routes is considerably longer than the others – a Brown-signposted route called the Backharn Trail, linking Nethy Bridge and Grantown. The signposting for this route starts at the Causer car park (*see* map).

The walk passes through woodland – both commercial conifer plantations and mature pine and birch woodland – and open ground, offering occasional fine views across Strathspey. It then passes through the grounds around Revack Lodge (*see* below) before joining the A95 a short distance south of Grantown.

The route is signposted both ways. If you are starting from Grantown, walk south on the A95, cross the river, then turn right onto the B970. The start of the walk is signposted to the left of the road almost at once.

Walk C) At Revack Lodge (entry off the B970) there is a garden centre, shop and tearoom. There are also six short to moderate walks laid out through the plantations and open ground around the buildings. The shortest of these is no more than half a mile; the longest – the Orange route – is five miles, and forms part of the BackharnTrail (*see* above).

1 *Carn Bheadhair (803m)* **2** *Bynack More (1090m)* **3** *Bynack Beg (964m)* **4** *Beinn Mheadhoin*
5 *Cairn Gorm (1245m)* **6** *Meall a' Bhuachaille (810m)* **7** *Creagan Gorm (732m)* **8** *Craiggowrie (686m)*

3 Nethy Bridge to Glenmore ————————————————— B

A long, lineal route following clear tracks through commercial and natural pine forest. Length: **10 miles/16km** (one way); *Height Climbed:* **650ft/190m** (north to south), **250ft/70m** (south to north).

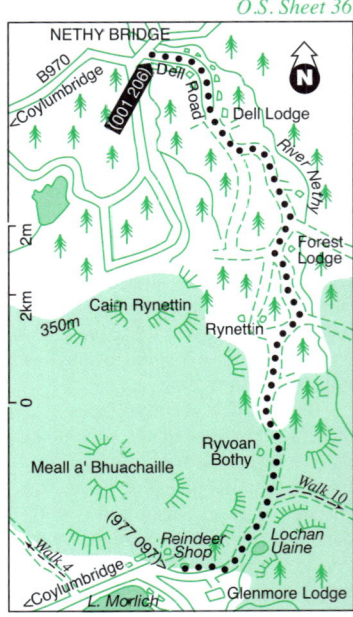

O.S. Sheet 36

Nethy Bridge is a small village to the east of the River Spey, 11 miles north of Coylumbridge on the B970. Start this walk from the bridge carrying the road over the River Nethy, and turn up Dell Road (to the south of the river). Follow this road for a little over a mile/1.6km until it reaches Dell Lodge. At this point the road becomes a forest track and continues through a dense conifer plantation.

After a short distance you reach a clear fork in the track marked by a stand of fire brooms. At this point go left, climbing onto a ridge and then swinging round to the right. After a mile/1.6km a track cuts off to the left: ignore this and continue to a junction in a clearing. Turn right here, following the sign for Forest Lodge, and climb up to pass the buildings at the Lodge.

Past the Lodge, the next two left turns lead to farm buildings. Take the third turn to the left, signposted for Glenmore and Loch Morlich. After a short distance there is a four-way junction. Turn left here. After a mile/1.6km a track cuts off behind and to the left. Ignore this and continue; the track now emerging from the dense woodland into an area of scattered pines, heather and juniper. At the next junction keep left (the right-hand track leads up past the buildings at Rynettin then back to Forest Lodge) and continue, with fine views of the Cairngorms ahead.

In the next band of conifers there is a further track cutting off to the left. Ignore this and continue: past Ryvoan Bothy and the end of the Loch Avon track (Walk 10), then on past little Lochan Uaine and Glenmore Lodge down to Glenmore, just by the reindeer centre.

4 Milton of Kincardine _____B

A short, lineal route across a low hill pass and passing through commercial forestry, pine woodland and open farmland.
Length: **4 miles/6.5km** (one way); *Height Climbed:* **165ft/50m** (south to north), **450ft/140m** (north to south).

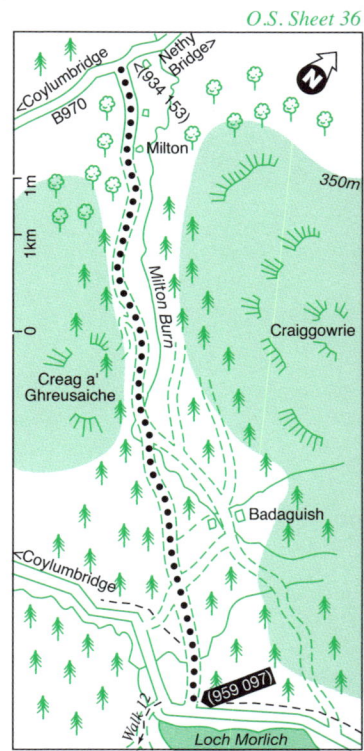

O.S. Sheet 36

To reach the start of the route, drive east from the southern end of Aviemore on the B970 road signposted for Cairngorm. At Coylumbridge, carry on towards Glenmore. Just as Loch Morlich starts to the right of the road, a clear track cuts off to the left, signposted for Milton of Kincardine. Park in one of the lochside car parks (fee) and start walking up the track, through conifer woodland.

There is little difficulty with the route: the junctions with other forestry tracks are as shown on the map, and the track climbs gently up to the narrow saddle between Creag a' Ghreusaiche and Craiggowrie. Just beyond the highest point of the saddle, the main track heads off to the left; for this route, however, keep to the right. Up to this point the route has passed through rather dull commercial forestry; beyond the saddle it becomes more interesting: passing through mature, scattered pine woodland at first, with heather and juniper amongst the undergrowth, and then through a hillocky grazing land of birch, bracken and grasses.

The difficulty with this route is the far end: a farm entrance (signposted for Kincardine Cottage), four miles north of Coylumbridge on the B970, with no nearby parking. Ideally, you should get someone to drop you here and walk back. One other possibility is a loop with Walk 3, via the quiet roads south of Loch Garten, though this would make for a long day's hike.

5 Aviemore to Carrbridge _____ A

A long, lineal route on generally clear tracks, passing across open moorland and farmland and through commercial forestry. Length: **19 miles/30.5km**; *Height Climbed:* **1650ft/500m**. *It is possible to make a circuit of this route, but the final part of the walk would be along a busy stretch of public road, and is therefore not recommended.*

O.S. Sheets 35 & 36

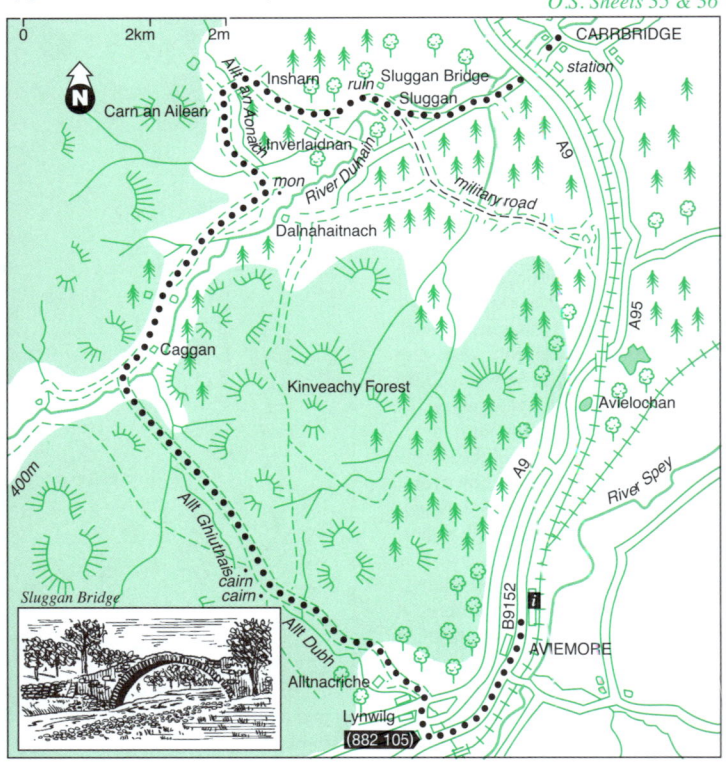

Walk south from Aviemore along the verge of the B9152. When the road reaches a junction, turn right on the road leading up to the A9. Cross the main road (carefully) and turn right. After a short distance turn left up the driveway signposted for Lynwilg.

Follow this metalled road over

a small bridge and then turn left up a private road signposted for Alltnacriche. Follow this road up a pleasant wooded glen until, just before Alltnacriche, a track heads right, signposted for Carrbridge. Climb through trees with a fence to the left at first, then continue across open moorland, with Allt Dubh in its narrow glen down to the left. The track, quite steep but perfectly clear, climbs on to a broad moorland ridge.

Where the track reaches the highest point of the route there is a cairn, and a rough path sets off behind and to the left. Ignore this and continue. At the far side of the ridge there is a second cairn and a path cuts off ahead and to the left. Ignore this also and continue along the clear track, down into the broad, heathery valley of Allt Ghiuthais.

Cross the burn on a bridge and continue beyond; climbing over a low ridge and then dropping down to a wooden bridge across the River Dulnain. Turn right at the far end of the bridge. At first the track is broad and clear; passing the cottage at Caggan and continuing. After about a mile/1.6km, however, it passes through a fence and then continues as a faint grassy path.

Continue on the rough path down the glen (eventually climbing on to the ridge above the flood plain) until the cottage at Dalnahaitnach is visible over the river. At this point, watch for a small stone monument to the right of the now clear track. Immediately beyond this, the track splits. Keep left, and follow the track north-west; over a footbridge across a small burn and on beyond. Ignore two tracks cutting off to the left and continue to the bridge over Allt an Aonaich. Turn right at the junction beyond this and continue, past the cottage at Insharn and on along a clear track with a conifer plantation to the left.

After a little under a mile/1.6km a clear track cuts off to the right (leading to Inverlaidnan). Ignore this and continue. A second, rougher path cuts off. Ignore this also and continue; climbing through woodland, then dropping down to the wonderful old hump-backed bridge over the River Dulnain at Sluggan (part of one of General Wade's eighteenth-century military roads). Cross the bridge and follow the track beyond up to a split. At this point you have a choice.

To reach Carrbridge go left and continue to join a minor road. Two miles/3.2km along this road (to the left) is the railway station, and a little beyond this the village itself. From here, there are public transport services leading back to Aviemore.

To reach Avielochan go right. When the track reaches the road go straight across. The old military road continues beyond; leading a further five miles/8km through conifer forestry and birch woodland to Avielochan, three miles/4.8km north of Aviemore. A good map will be needed to navigate through the various tracks in the conifer section, and the final walk along the busy A95/B9152 is not recommended.

6 Meall a' Bhuachaille — B

A steep hill climb through woodland and open moorland, leading to excellent views. Can be either a there-and-back climb or a longer loop.
Length: 3-5 miles/5-8km; **Height Climbed: 1550ft/480m**.

O.S. Sheet 36

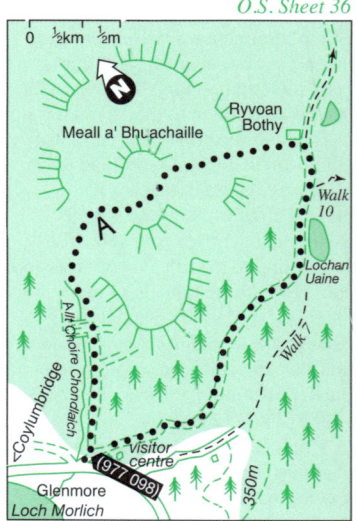

To reach the start of the route, turn east from the southern end of Aviemore on the B970 road signposted for Cairngorm. After two miles the road reaches a junction at Coylumbridge: carry straight on to Glenmore, a short distance beyond the end of Loch Morlich. There are a number of parking places in and around Glenmore.

To start the route, walk up to the back of Glenmore Visitor Centre and look for a path marked by a sign for the walk. This path climbs steeply to a T-junction. Turn left here, still on a clear path, and climb through the conifer woodland with Allt Choire Chondlaich in a deep valley to your left. Continue until you reach the edge of the trees.

The path remains clear beyond: climbing through open heather moorland to a col between Creagan Gorm and Meall a' Bhuachaille. Turn right to reach the summit.

For the shorter return, retrace your steps. For a slightly longer walk, head east from the summit, following a rough path down a steep slope to reach Ryvoan Bothy. Turn right here on a clear track; passing Lochan Uaine and returning to the start on the Blue way-marked forest walk (*see Walk 7*).

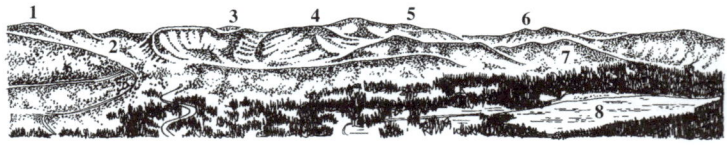

1 *Cairn Gorm (1245m)* **2** *Ski Slopes* **3** *Cairnlochan (1215m)* **4** *Creag an Leth-choin (1053m)*
5 *Braeriach (1296m)* **6** *Sgor Gaoith (1118m)* **7** *Carn Eilrig (742m)* **8** *Loch Morlich*

7 Five Glenmore Forest Walks   C

Five signposted walks through pine woodland and forestry on clear tracks. Length: 1¼, 1½, 2½, 3½ *and* 3½ **miles/2.2, 2.4, 3.9, 5.8** *and* **5.8km**; *Height Climbed:* up to **350ft/100m** (Blue route).

O.S. Sheet 36

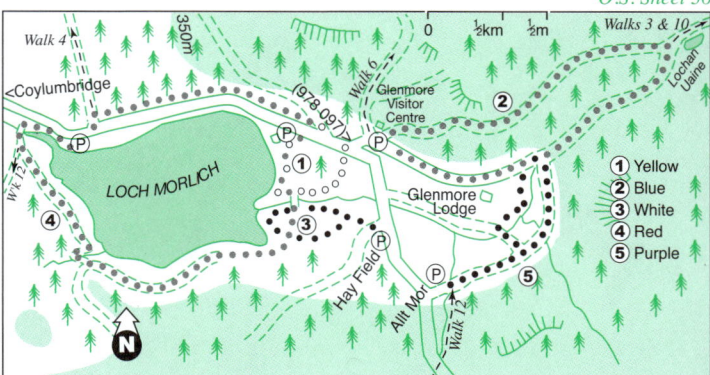

These short, waymarked circuits are the easiest introduction to the beautiful woodland surrounding Loch Morlich. To reach the routes, turn east from the southern end of Aviemore on the B970 road for Cairngorm. Carry straight on at the junction at Coylumbridge and drive on up to Glenmore, just beyond the end of Loch Morlich. The walks start from three car parks in and beyond Glenmore (*see* map).

Glenmore: Many first time visitors will choose to visit the information centre at Glenmore to get their bearings. Two waymarked walks can be started from the car park here. The **Yellow** route (1½ miles) leads down to the sandy beach by Loch Morlich, then back through the woods by Allt Mor. This also provides a link with the **Red** route (3½ miles), which makes a circuit of the loch. If you want more of a climb, the **Blue** route (3½ miles) leads up to the green waters of little Lochan Uaine in the Ryvoan Pass.

Hay Field: One short walk – **White** (1¼ miles) – makes a circuit through the woods by Allt Mor, while there is also a link to the longer **Red** route (3½ miles) around the loch.

Allt Mor: One walk starts from here – the **Purple** route (2½ miles) – which makes a circuit through the conifer woods about Allt Mor and its tributaries, and links with the **Blue** route leading to Lochan Uaine.

A detailed leaflet describing these routes is available locally, and there are maps at the various starting points showing the available options.

8 Coylumbridge_____B

An easy circuit along rough, clear footpaths and tracks, passing through conifer woodland and open heather moorland. Length: **4½ miles/7km**; *Height Climbed:* **250ft/70m**.

O.S. Sheet 36

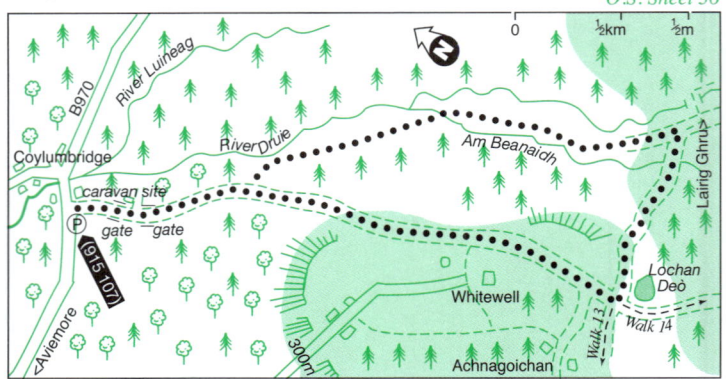

To reach Coylumbridge, turn east from the southern end of Aviemore on the B970 and follow it for around two miles. Shortly before the junction of the Nethy Bridge and Cairngorm roads there is a long lay-by to the right of the road. Park here.

Start walking up the broad track which exits the lay-by, passing a caravan site. After a short distance there is a gate. Go through this, past a ruined building, then straight on to reach a second gate. Beyond this continue, through conifer woodland, for about half a mile/0.8km to reach a fork in the track. The junction is signposted: left for Lairig Ghru; right for Glen Einich. Keep to the left, and follow the clear track through an area of open grassland and scattered trees, with the River Druie a short distance to the left, before entering denser woodland once again.

Continue up to a clear junction. Straight ahead is the way to the Lairig Ghru (Walk 12). For this route, however, turn right at the junction (cutting back at a sharp angle) following a sign for Loch an Eilein.

Walk half a mile/0.8km, through mixed woodland and moorland, to a further signposted junction just beyond little Lochan Deò. A turn to the left at this point leads up to Loch Einich (Walk 14), while Loch an Eilein is about a mile/1.6km directly ahead (Walk 13). For this route, however, turn right and, ignoring tracks leading up to the left, continue on a clear track through open moorland and juniper scrub back to the fork near the start of the walk.

9 Inverdruie — B

Complicated but gentle circuit along low-lying roads, tracks and footpaths, through woodland, moorland and farmland. Length: **7 miles/11km**; Height Climbed: **300ft/90m**.

O.S. Sheet 36

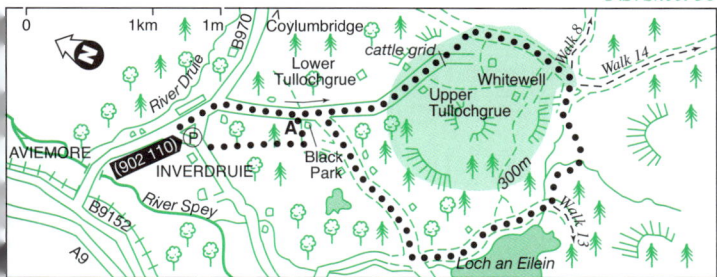

To reach Inverdruie, turn east from the southern end of Aviemore on the B970 and follow it for a mile until the road to Feshiebridge cuts off to the right. Turn onto this, then first left, into the car park.

Start walking along the B970, continuing through Inverdruie in the direction of Coylumbridge. After a short distance turn right onto the minor road signposted for Black Park, which climbs gently through mixed woodland. After a little under a mile/1.6km a path cuts across the way (A). (To the left this leads to Coylumbridge). Carry straight on. A short distance beyond there is a fork in the road at Black Park. Go left, on the road signposted for Tullochgrue.

The road passes between fields then crosses a cattle grid. Head left immediately on a track through heather and juniper scrub to join a clear track at the foot of the slope. Turn right along this and carry straight on until, after a mile/1.6km, a signposted four-way junction is reached. Turn right at this point, on the track for Loch an Eilein. Ignore tracks cutting off to the right and left and carry on across moorland and through scattered pine woodland until you join a clear track. Turn right along this (signposted for Aviemore) and continue until it reaches the end of the public road leading to the car park by the loch. Turn right off the public road, almost immediately, and follow a clear track through farmland and woodland back to Black Park.

Turn back down the public road, but at the junction (A) turn left, around a gate, onto a rough path through pine woodland. After 250 paces an unsignposted path heads off to the right. Turn onto this and follow it – through trees at first, then across an open area, then finally through a dense conifer plantation – back to the car park.

10 Loch Avon ──────────────────────── A+

*A long, demanding loop across open moorland on tracks and rough, damp footpaths, leading to a small loch in the heart of the Cairngorms. Length: **21 miles/34km**; Height Climbed: **1550ft/470m**. Quite gruelling, and not for the inexperienced. Care should be taken to be fully equipped for the walk, to advise someone of the route being taken, and to take note of the weather forecast.*

O.S. Sheet 36

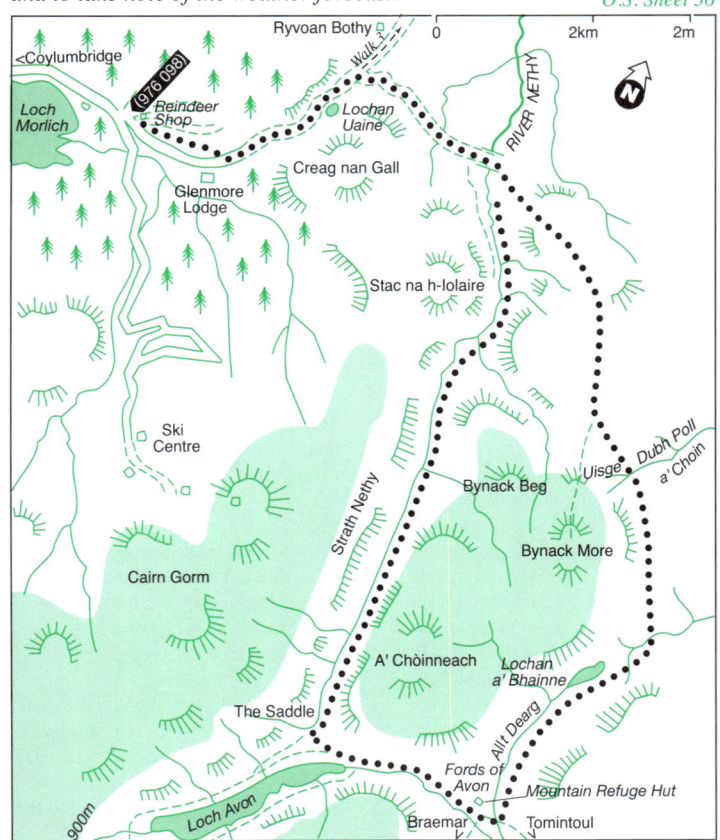

This is a splendid walk – leading round the eastern flank of the Cairngorms – but it is also a long one, and lacks any obvious 'escape routes'. Take particular care, therefore, to ensure that correct maps and equipment are carried in order to avoid unnecessary dangers.

To reach the start of the route, turn east from the southern end of Aviemore on the B970 road signposted for Cairngorm. Continue beyond Coylumbridge along the road for Glenmore. There are parking places in and around Glenmore.

Start walking up the cyclist/walkers' track past the Reindeer shop. Follow this until it joins the metalled road beyond Glenmore Lodge, then continue. When the tarmac ends a clear forestry track continues. Follow this; climbing up through pine woodland to Lochan Uaine in its narrow pass, and then on to a split in the track shortly beyond.

Take the right-hand path, signposted for Braemar, and follow it through heather moorland around the foot of Creag nan Gall and Stac na h-Iolaire until, after a little over a mile/1.6km, you reach a bridge over the River Nethy. Cross this.

Immediately beyond it a rough path cuts off to the right. Ignore this and carry straight on; following a rough but clear track up the slope ahead. The path climbs up to a plateau (where the path forks, with the right-hand path climbing Bynack More), before dropping to cross the headwaters of Uisge Dubh Poll a' Choin, rising to cross a further low ridge, and then dropping once more into a narrow glen. The path is very clear at this point; dropping down to the bottom of the glen and then continuing along the far side; passing two small lochs, then crossing the burn (Allt Dearg) before reaching the Mountain Refuge Hut at fords of Avon.

At this point there is a four-way junction. The track to the left is the start of a long walk down the Avon to Tomintoul; the route straight ahead (if the river is fordable) leads through Lairig an Laoigh to Derry Lodge and Braemar (neither of these routes should be attempted without careful preparation). For this walk, however, turn right; following a wet, rough path leading up the right-hand side of the river into the heart of the hills. After a mile/1.6km the path reaches Loch Avon, surrounded by spectacular peaks.

From the near end of the loch, a wet, rocky path climbs diagonally up the slope to the right. Follow this up to The Saddle: a low col beneath the steep slopes of Cairn Gorm. On the watershed the path is joined by another climbing up from further along Loch Avon. Ignore this and swing right; dropping down into the head of Strath Nethy. The path is damp at first; then rougher but drier as it leads down the right-hand side of the burn through the narrow, rocky, treeless glen. Follow the track down to the bridge over the River Nethy and then return by the original track.

Walks Aviemore

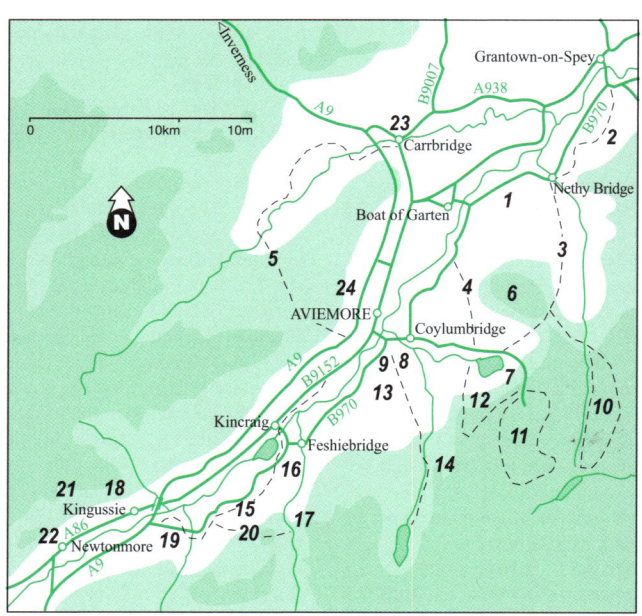

Local and topographic terms

Allt – Burn, stream
Beinn, ben – Mountain
Bothy – Hut
Carn, cairn – Hill, heap of stones
Coire – Corrie (hollow)

Creag, craig – Rock, steep hill
Lairig – Hill pass
Lochan – Small loch
Stac – Rocky column, cliff
Strath – Valley

— www.pocketwalks.com —

Published by: Hallewell Publications, Scotland
Printed by: Barr Printers, Glenrothes

Walks Aviemore

walk	grade	walk	grade
1 Loch Garten	C	13 Loch an Eilein	C
2 Nethy Bridge & Grantown	B/C	14 Loch Einich	A
3 Nethy Bridge to Glenmore	B	15 The Badenoch Way	A/B/C
4 Milton of Kincardine	B	16 Feshiebridge & Uath Lochans	C
5 Aviemore to Carrbridge	A	17 Upper Glen Feshie	B
6 Meall a' Bhuachaille	B	18 Creag Bheag	B
7 Five Glenmore Forest Walks	C	19 Ruthven to Glen Tromie	B
8 Coylumbridge	B	20 Drumguish to Glen Feshie	B
9 Inverdruie	B	21 Kingussie to Newtonmore	B
10 Loch Avon	A+	22 Newtonmore	B
11 Cairn Gorm	A+	23 Carrbridge	C
12 Loch Morlich to Lairig Ghru	A	24 Craigellachie	B/C

Grades

A+ .... Full walking equipment – including map and compass – and previous hill walking experience essential

A ...... Full walking equipment required

B ...... Strong footwear and waterproof clothing required

C ...... Comfortable footwear recommended

While every care has been taken in the preparation of this guide, the publishers cannot accept responsibility for any loss, damage or injury resulting from its use.

11 Cairn Gorm   A+

A straight hill climb, with clear footpaths on the lower, moorland section, although care is required with the navigation on the open plateau. Length: **8 miles/13km**; *Height Climbed:* **2000ft/600m**. *Steep cliff edges to the plateau; great care needed in poor visibility.*

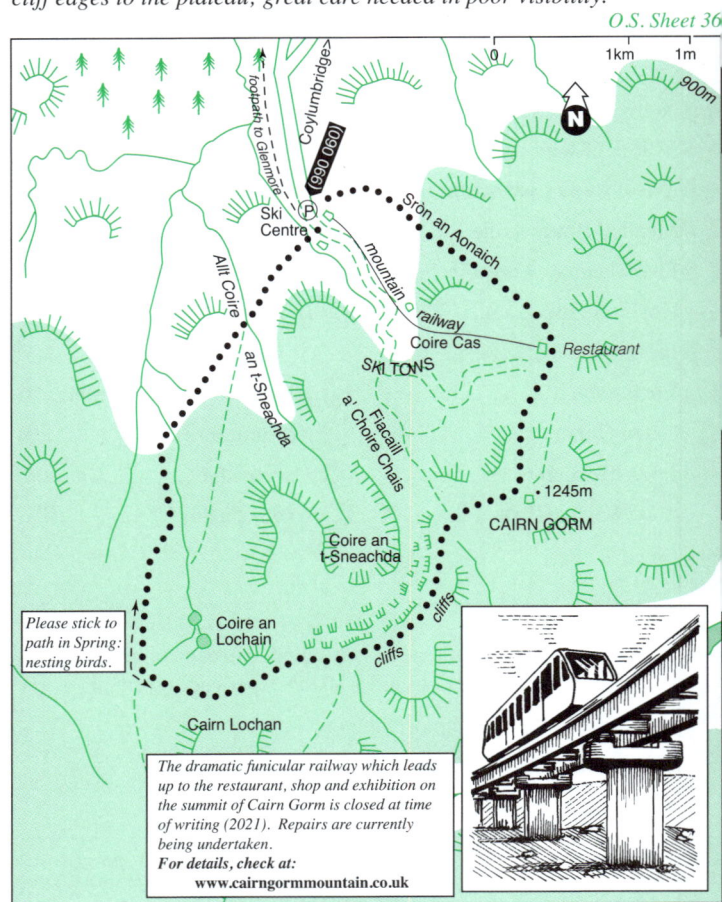

O.S. Sheet 36

Please stick to path in Spring: nesting birds.

The dramatic funicular railway which leads up to the restaurant, shop and exhibition on the summit of Cairn Gorm is closed at time of writing (2021). Repairs are currently being undertaken.
For details, check at:
www.cairngormmountain.co.uk

The peaks of the Cairngorms constitute one of the most popular areas for hill-walking in Scotland. Given good weather the mountain landscape is comparatively benign and outstandingly beautiful. Nevertheless, this is a potentially dangerous environment, and great care should always be taken when walking on the tops (*see* inside front cover). This particular walk follows a comparatively short climb onto the plateau.

To reach the start of the climb, turn east from the southern end of Aviemore on the B970, signposted for Cairngorm. Follow the road past Loch Morlich and up to the car park for the ski slopes at Coire Cas. Walk up to the first of the buildings at the upper end of the car park and look for a clear path setting off to the right (south-west) at this point. Follow this across the open moorland, with fine views, down to Loch Morlich and Aviemore. Cross Allt Coire an t-Sneachda and climb the slope beyond. After a short distance the path splits, with one branch climbing due south into Coire an Lochain. Ignore this and carry straight on; crossing a further burn and then swinging left on a clear path which can be seen ahead climbing up the inside of the ridge to the west of the corrie.

From the head of the corrie, the path climbs onto the broad plateau. At this point navigation becomes more complicated, and great care, as well as some work with a map and compass, may be necessary: particularly if, as is so often the case, visibility is poor.

Southwards lies the peak of Ben Macdui – the highest point in the Cairngorms. For this route, however, turn left and follow a rough path up the edge of the corrie to the peak of Cairn Lochan, then follow the cliff-edges beyond; swinging northwards towards the peak of Cairn Gorm. Great care must be taken on this stage of the walk, and no amount of description will act as a substitute for a good map, a compass, and the ability to use both. From the peak to the south of Cairn Gorm there is a choice of paths, with one path heading down the ridge of Fiacall a' Choire Chais, to the west of the ski slopes, and the other climbing to the peak of Cairn Gorm. From the peak, a clear path leads down past the restaurant at the head of the funicular railway. Walk on beyond this, down the ridge of Sròn an Aonaich, before dropping down to the west to return to the car park.

The Cairngorms from Craigellachie (Walk 24)
1 *Cairn Gorm (1245m)* **2** *Ben Macdui (1309m)* **3** *Lairig Ghru* **4** *Sron na Lairige (1180m)*
5 *Braeriach (1235m)* **6** *Creag Dhubh (848m)*

12 Loch Morlich to Lairig Ghru ——————————————A

A long loop on clear tracks and rough footpaths, climbing through pinewood and open moorland to the start of the Lairig Ghru pass, then returning via a scramble through a dramatic rocky gully. Length: **12 miles/19km**; *Height Climbed:* **1250ft/380m**.

O.S. Sheet 36

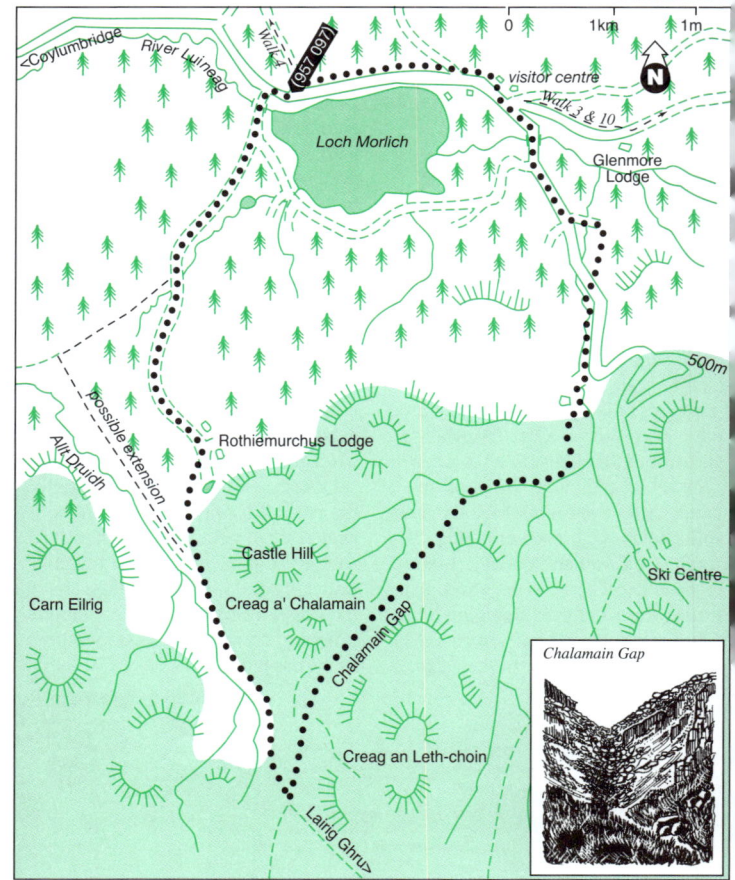

Chalamain Gap

To reach the start of this route, drive east from the southern end of Aviemore along the B970 road signposted for Cairngorm. Continue on the minor road past Coylumbridge up to Loch Morlich. There are numerous parking places by the side of Loch Morlich, in Glenmore and beyond. Park in one of them and then walk back down the road towards Coylumbridge.

Just beyond the end of Loch Morlich, a track cuts off to the left, leading to a bridge over the River Luineag, at the point where it exits the loch. Cross this and continue along the forestry track beyond. When a track cuts off to the left, carry straight on. After a further mile/1.6km there is a second split. The right-hand track (signposted for 'Picadilly') joins up with other routes through Rothiemurchus Forest (Walk 8), and also provides an alternative, and slightly longer, section of this route (*see* map). Otherwise, keep to the left at the junction, along the track signposted for Rothiemurchus Lodge.

The track is clear at first; climbing up towards the lodge. At the lodge, look for a bell to your right and turn right on a path just before it. The path climbs steeply to reach a small reservoir, passes to the right of it and continues. Follow this path, through heather moorland and stunted pine trees, to a junction by the edge of the glen of Allt Druidh. The path coming in from the right is the end of the 'Picadilly' diversion. For this route, however, go left: climbing up the lip of the glen through open moorland, with the entrance to the Lairig Ghru – the long, testing track which leads through the Cairngorms to Braemar – directly ahead. (Please note, this longer route is a serious proposition, even for experienced hill-walkers, and should not be considered without careful attention being paid to maps, equipment and general planning.)

After a little over a mile/1.6km, as the hills begin to crowd in on either side, a rough path cuts off back and to the left. Turn onto this, and follow it up the slope to the gap between Creag an Leth-choin and Creag a' Chalamain. Between the two is a deep gully, filled with granite boulders, called the Chalamain Gap. Clamber through this (taking great care; it is easy to twist an ankle between the rocks) and continue along a dry path through heather and pine saplings beyond.

The path drops down to the side of a small burn, then clambers up the far side. Continue along the path beyond; eventually dropping back down a steep slope to the burn, which is crossed at this point by a footbridge. Cross this and turn left along a clear, rough path to reach the public road.

Entrance to the Lairig Ghru

13 Loch an Eilein _____ C

A charming circuit on clear tracks through the pine woodland surrounding a small loch. Length: **4 miles/6.5km**; *Height Climbed:* negligible. *There is a ruined castle on the island in the middle of the loch.*

O.S. Sheet 36

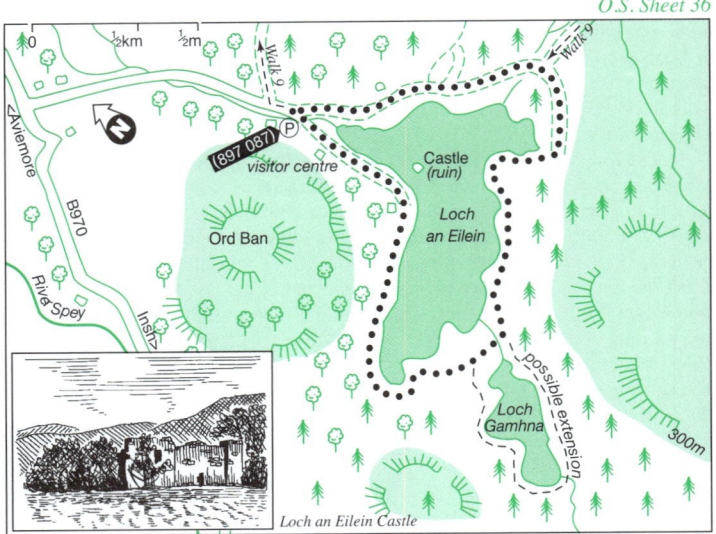

Loch an Eilein Castle

To reach the start of the route, turn east from the southern end of Aviemore onto the B970 road signposted for Cairngorm. After a little under a mile, turn right onto the road signposted for Insh. After a further mile, turn left onto the minor road signposted for Loch an Eilein. At the end of the public road there is a car park (a charge is levied).

Walk straight on, beyond the end of the car park, past the small shop and on to the lochside. The route around the loch is perfectly clear (the track itself splits from time to time, but it is difficult to get lost with the loch shore for guidance); passing through birch, larch and pine woodland, and providing views of the ruins of the 14th-century castle on the island in the loch.

There is one obvious possible extension to this route – making an additional loop of around a mile/1.6km around Loch Gamhna to the south of the loch. Otherwise, the paths around Loch an Eilein are connected with the mass of footpaths in and around Rothiemurchus (*see* Walks 8,9,12 and 14).

14 Loch Einich _____ A

A long, lineal route on clear tracks, leading to a loch ringed by steep hills. Length: up to **16 miles/25.5km** (there and back)*; Height Climbed:* **650ft/200m**.

O.S. Sheet 36

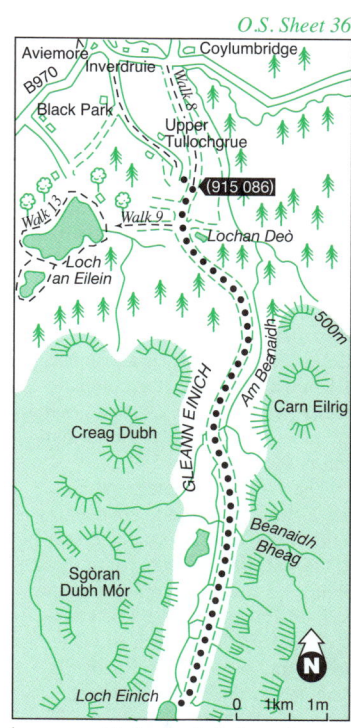

This walk starts amidst the net of interconnecting footpaths between Loch an Eilein and Loch Morlich. As such, it can be started from a variety of places; most obviously Loch an Eilein (Walk 13), Inverdruie (Walk 9), Coylumbridge (Walk 8), and Loch Morlich (Walk 12). For the shortest route, however, turn east from the southern end of Aviemore onto the B970 road for Cairngorm. After a mile the road reaches Inverdruie. Ignore the first turn to the right (to Feshiebridge), and take the second, minor, road for Black Park. At the fork in the road keep left, and climb up from the woodland onto the open farmland and moorland above. Continue to the car park at the end of the road, then walk down the clear path which drops down to join the clear track lower down the hill (part of Walk 8). Swing right along this and continue through a mixture of pine woodland and moorland up to the four-way junction at Lochan Deò. The tracks are signposted: carry straight on along the Loch Einich track, through heather moorland and scattered Scots pine woodland.

The route is not in any doubt – the track soon joins Am Beanaidh (the river flowing from Loch Einich) and simply follows it up the glen – but there can be difficulties in damp weather, since a number of smaller burns need to be forded along the way (Beanaidh Bheag, in particular, is virtually impassable when in spate). Given good weather, however, it is worth the effort, as the corrie of Loch Einich – the loch surrounded by ranks of cliffs, scree slopes and higher corries – is particularly splendid.

Return by the same route.

15 The Badenoch Way — A/B/C

A pleasant series of connected roads, tracks and footpaths through open and wooded country in the Spey Valley. Well signposted. Possible links with Walks 19 and 20. **Length: 10 miles/16km** *(one way); Height Climbed: undulating. Can be walked in short sections.*

O.S. Sheet 35

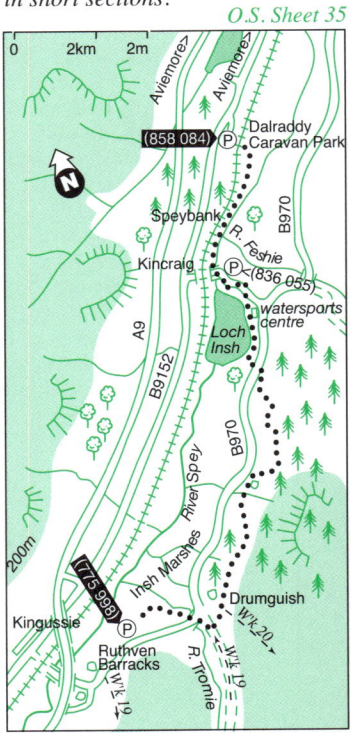

The Badenoch Way links Dalraddy in the north (starting from the car park at the caravan site, 3 miles south of Aviemore on the B9152) with the RSPB car park at Insh Marshes in the south (2 miles east of Kingussie on the B970). There is no room here to describe the route in detail, but the numerous junctions are extremely well signposted in both directions. This should allow you to follow short sections without further assistance; if you wish to follow the complete walk, mark the route on your OS map (there are route maps at the car parks) before starting.

The Way as a whole provides a fascinating, and not too challenging, tour. If you have no time to complete it, the walk can be joined at numerous points (*see* map); the prime sections being the woodland walk between Speybank and Loch Insh and the nature trail between the RSPB car park and Tromie Bridge, with its hides overlooking the Insh Marshes.

There is one shop along the route (at Kincraig), and it is possible to get refreshments at the Watersports Centre by Loch Insh.

There are railway stations at both Aviemore and Kingussie, plus bus links, so it is possible to walk one way and ride back. Another possibility is to link the walk with one of the other routes in the book (*see* map). Walk 19 provides a short loop, using a section of the Way. A longer loop can be made using Walk 20 and the Glen Feshie road (*see* OS 35).

16 Feshiebridge & Uath Lochans _____C

Two sets of waymarked forest walks: one group centred on the River Feshie, the other on a steep, wooded crag above a cluster of small lochans. **Lengths:** 1¼ **miles/2km** to 2½ **miles/4km**. **Height Climbed:** various, most low-level.

O.S. Sheet 35

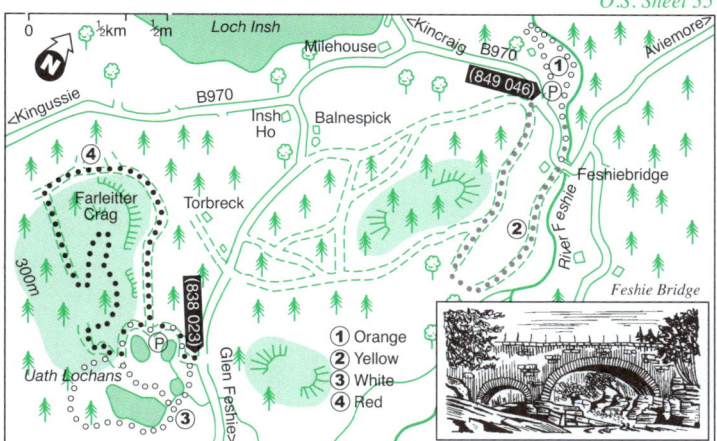

To reach the start of these routes, drive six miles north from Kingussie on the B9152 road. When the road reaches the village of Kincraig, turn right onto a minor road which crosses the Spey north of Loch Insh. After about a mile you reach a T-junction with the B970.

To reach the Feshiebridge walks, turn left. After a short distance there is a car park to the left of the road. Two colour-coded walks start from the car park – Orange and Yellow – following the shallow River Feshie as it flows through the woods. The river is notable for its extensive, ever-shifting gravel banks.

To reach the Uath Lochans walks, turn right, then first left up a minor road for Glen Feshie. After about a mile a track heads right to the car park.

From here there are two walks. The White walk is a low-level route through the conifer woodland around a cluster of small lochans. The Red walk (if walked anti-clockwise) starts through regular forestry woodland then ends dramatically on the low, craggy escarpment of Farleitter Crag, from where there are terrific views out across the lochs and trees below.

Maps showing the routes can be seen in the two car parks.

17 Upper Glen Feshie _____B

A loop in the open, upper part of Glen Feshie; partly on a quiet, metalled road and partly on rough, damp footpaths. Length: **9 miles/ 14.5km**; *Height Climbed:* **175ft/50m**.

O.S. Sheet 35

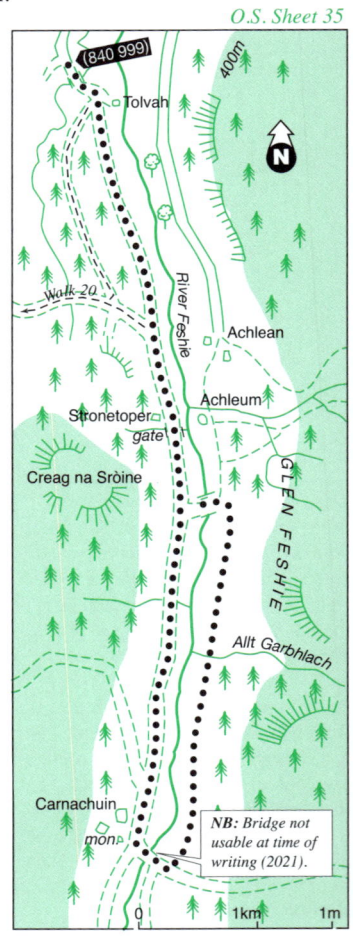

Glen Feshie is a long, narrow valley flanking the western edge of the Cairngorms; taking waters from the high mountains and the wastes of Badenoch and channelling them northwards to enter the Spey near Kincraig. The upper part of the glen is surrounded by bleak moorland, though it also includes remnants of the old pine woods of the area.

To reach the upper glen, follow the directions shown for the Uath Lochans car park (Walk 16), but continue beyond the car park for a further two miles to the conclusion of the metalled road. Park before or after the small bridge.

Walk on beyond, keeping right at the first fork and left at the second, then continuing through conifer woodland to the cottage at Stronetoper. Shortly beyond the cottage there is a bridge over the river to the left. Cross this and follow a series of footpaths running parallel to the river, through moorland and woodland, for a further two miles/ 3.2km.

You pass the obvious white lodge at Carnachuin on the far bank then close with the river to look for the footbridge. At time of writing (2021), this bridge is missing. If it is still missing, return by your original route; otherwise cross over and double back down the far side of the glen.

18 Creag Bheag ──────────────────────────────B

A short hill climb over rough ground, leading to fine views of Strathspey and the surrounding hills. Length: **3½ miles/5.5km**; *Height Climbed:* **900ft/270m**.

O.S. Sheet 35

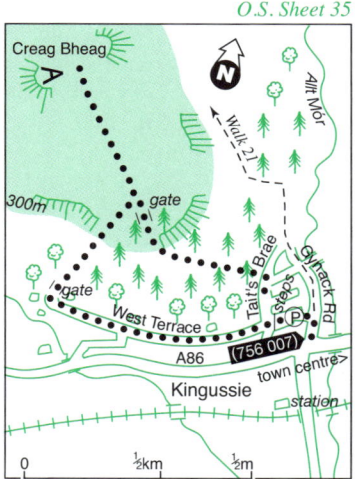

To the north-west of Kingussie town centre is the bald, rocky head of Creag Bheag, rising up above a fringe of conifer and broad-leaved woodland. The climb to the summit is steep but short; the resulting views are excellent.

Park in the centre of the town. There is a free car park a short distance up Gynack Road, to the west of Allt Mór (*see map*). Walk out of the back of the car park and on across a small park. Climb the steps at the far side of the park, leading up to the public road (Tait's Brae). Cross this road and continue along West Terrace, following a sign for 'West Terrace Circular'. Continue to the end of this road, and then carry on along a driveway which swings up to the right. Just before the final house is reached, turn up a grass track leading to a gate. Go through the gate and swing right, at a purple waymarker for Creag Bheag, on a rough path through open woodland of birch and juniper.

Within a few paces there is a fence to your right with a conifer plantation beyond it and birch woodland and moorland climbing to your left. After a short climb a rough, signposted path leads off to the left, climbing up to the long summit of the hill.

Return by the same path. At the signposted junction, take the left-hand path to reach a gate into the conifer plantation and follow a rough path through the trees down to Tait's Brae. Turn right to return to the start.

1 *Beinn Udlaman (1010m)* **2** *Cruban Beag (590m)* **3** *Beinn Bheoh (1016m)* **4** *Meall Liath (911m)*
5 *Geal Charn (1132m)* **6** *Geal Charn (1049m)* **7** *Newtonmore* **8** *Creag Dhubh (717m)* **9** *Carn Liath (1006m)*
10 *Marg na Craige (834m)*

19 Ruthven to Glen Tromie /
20 Drumguish to Glen Feshie ——————— B/B

Two short hill crossings of differing character: the first starting on occasionally rough and damp footpaths over the open hill (some navigation may be necessary), and returning through Insh Marshes Nature Reserve; the second following clear moorland footpaths and tracks through conifer woodland. **19)** *Length:* **6½ miles/10.5km** (complete circuit); *Height Climbed:* **650ft/200m**. **20)** *Length:* **5 miles/8km** (one way); *Height Climbed:* **350ft/100m**.

O.S. Sheet 35

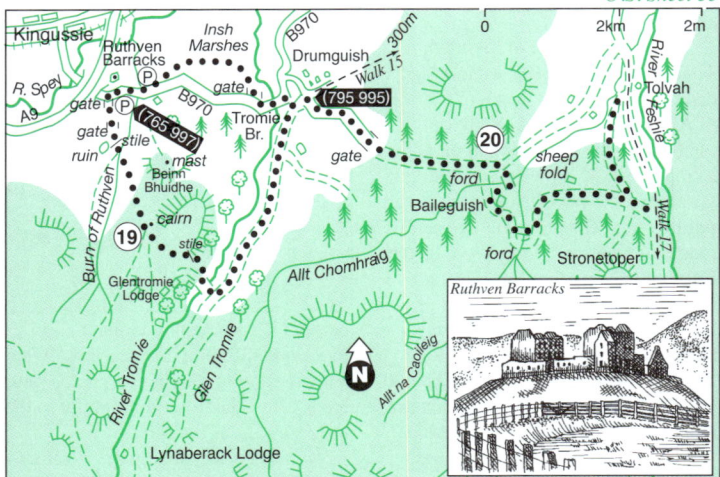

Glen Feshie, on the western edge of the Cairngorms, and Glen Tromie, running parallel to the west, carry tributary streams of the River Spey northwards through heather hills and forestry. The tracks to the east of Glen Feshie are severe, but those linking the two glens, and linking Glen Tromie to Kingussie, are gentler.

Walk 19) To start this route from Kingussie, walk south from the centre of the town on the minor road signposted for Ruthven Barracks: the imposing ruin of an 18th-century military structure about a mile away on the far side of the valley. Alternatively, there is a car park at the Barracks themselves.

From the car park, walk back towards Kingussie. Almost immediately there are two gates in the fence at the top of the slope to the left of the road. Go through the right-hand gate and follow the clear track up the left-hand side of a field, go through a further gate and swing right. At the corner of the field turn left again, following a clear track up towards a wooded gap in the slope ahead. Pass through this gap and continue to the ruined cottage beyond.

There is a fence round the cottage. Walk up the left-hand edge of this fence to reach a tall stile by a gate in a deer fence, leading onto the open hill. Follow the grassy path beyond this.

The path is very faint at first, but after crossing the Burn of Ruthven it is not in doubt, as it climbs towards a dip in the hills to the right of Beinn Bhuidhe (the hill with the radio mast).

A little short of the watershed a low cairn marks a junction. Ignore the faint, old track to your right. Just beyond the cairn there is a second split. Keep ahead-left here, crossing the watershed then descending into Glen Tromie.

The path leads to a tall stile over a deer fence, with birch woodland beyond. Cross the stile and follow a rough path down through the trees, keeping left at the only junction to reach the corner of a deer fence. (If there is no corner in the fence you have missed the junction. Turn left along the fence to find the corner.)

From the corner, continue with the deer fence to your right and buildings beyond that. After a short distance there is a tall stile over the fence to the right. Cross this and continue a short distance along a vehicle track to a bridge over the River Tromie.

Once on the far side of the river, a rough road leads down the quiet glen to join the B970 at Tromie Bridge (to link with Walk 20, turn right just before the public road on a track signposted for the Badenoch Way).

Cross Tromie Bridge. At the far end, the Badenoch Way is signposted through a gate to the right. Follow the clear track beyond through the Nature Reserve to reach a car park, then follow the track by the public road to return to the start.

Walk 20) From the crossroads at the centre of the hamlet, follow the rough track signposted for Glen Feshie; quickly passing through a gate then continuing along a clear track across open moorland. When the track reaches the edge of a conifer plantation, pass through a gate and continue along the forest track beyond for two miles/3.2km, ignoring paths to left and right, until it emerges from the trees by Allt Chomhraig.

At this point, look for the ford and footbridge over the burn. Cross the bridge and head right to rejoin the rough track. Go left along this, passing to the right of the ruin at Baileguish and continuing to the ford/footbridge over Allt na Caoileig.

Beyond this the track continues, swinging right to pass an old sheep fold then running on to enter an area of commercial forestry.

After a mile/1.6km, the track reaches a signposted junction. The tracks straight ahead and back-left link with Walk 17 (*see* map).

21 Kingussie to Newtonmore — B

A lineal route linking neighbouring villages, passing through woodland and open moorland, and along the side of a small loch. Length: **4½ miles/7km** *(one way); Height Climbed:* **390ft/120m**. *Possible links with Walks 18 and 22.*

O.S. Sheet 35

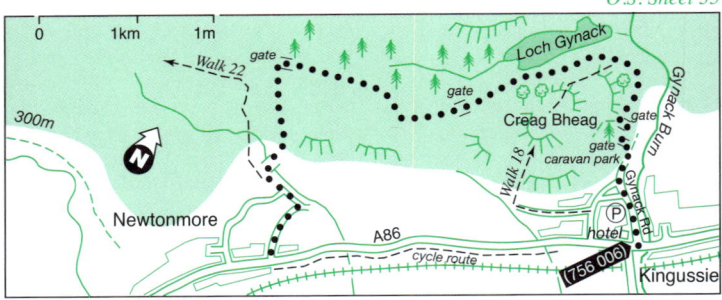

From the main street in Kingussie, turn up Gynack Road (beside the Duke of Gordon Hotel). There is a car park a short way up the road.

Continue walking up Gynack Road (there are also paths by the Gynack Burn, to your right) until it ends at the entrance to a caravan park. Walk a short way into the caravan park and you reach a junction, with a track heading left signposted for Newtonmore and Creag Bheag.

Turn left here and walk a short distance to reach a gate on the edge of the site. Go through this and turn right, with trees to your left and the caravans, initially, to your right.

After a short distance the fence to your left turns left and the path follows it, quickly reaching a gate in a deer fence. Go through this then keep right at the junction just beyond (Creag Bheag).

The rough, clear path leads around the end of Creag Bheag, with Loch Gynack becoming visible down to your right. At the next signposted junction you keep straight on (a turn to the left leads you up Creag Bheag – see Walk 18), on a rough path through birch trees, with the loch down to your right.

The loch ends and you continue on a clear path, marked by posts, with a part-felled conifer wood now visible on the far side of the shallow glen. Go through a gate in a deer fence and continue. Half way along the length of the conifer plantation the path turns hard right and heads towards it.

Follow the edge of the plantation, with the trees to your right, until you reach a gate level with its end. Go through this and head off half-left on a clear path which leads straight down to Newtonmore, visible below.

22 Newtonmore   B

A circuit on clear tracks and faint footpaths across low-lying, grassy moorland. Length: **6 miles/9.5km**; *Height Climbed:* **450ft/130m**.

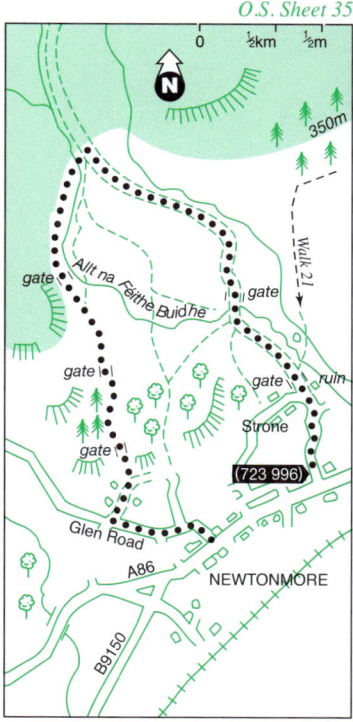

O.S. Sheet 35

This walk ventures onto the low moorland on the fringe of the Monadhliath Mountains, to the north of the pleasant town of Newtonmore. To start the route, walk up towards the northern end of the town (ie, in the direction of Kingussie) and turn left up the road signposted for Strone. This road climbs gently through farmland before swinging to the left to return to Newtonmore. At this point there is a small ruin to the right of the road with a gate beside it. Pass through this gate, and then a second a short distance beyond. The track forks: keep left and walk on along a clear track parallel to the burn.

After half a mile/0.8km the track drops to cross Allt na Féithe Buidhe and a path cuts off to the left. Ignore this and continue on the main track, which now swings off to the right before curving back to rejoin the burn as it emerges from its narrow upper glen. Cross the burn at this point and turn left. There is no path here and some navigation is needed: continue parallel to the burn for a short way until you reach a gate in a fence which crosses the way. Beyond this, the way becomes clearer.

A faint path continues by the burn for a short distance before heading off across the moorland to the right. Looking ahead, there is a low hill covered by birch trees, with a conifer plantation to its right. Aim for the left-hand edge of the conifer plantation (passing through a gate on the way). This leads to a gate in a fence beyond which a rough track leads across an open area to join a track providing access to a group of houses. Turn right along this track to reach a junction, then turn left, down Glen Road, to return to the town.

23 Carrbridge ─────────────────────── C

Three short, waymarked walks through attractive mixed woodland.
Lengths: up to **2½ miles/4km**; *Height Climbed:* negligible.

There are three possible start points, with maps, for these linked walks. Park either in the main village car park or in the woodland car park off Station Road and start walking.

The Red and Yellow routes are loops through the pleasant conifer woodland around the village. The Blue route is a lineal walk, starting

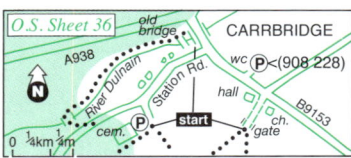

by the picturesque old bridge over the River Dulnain then following the river to join Station Road.

24 Craigellachie ─────────────────── B/C

Four waymarked walks through an area of protected birch woodland.
The longest is a lineal climb to a fine viewpoint. Length: up to
3 miles/5km (to summit and back); *Height Climbed:* up to **820ft/250m**.

From the centre of Aviemore, walk south along the main street. As the buildings begin to thin, look for a signpost to your right for the Youth Hostel and Nature Reserve. Turn right on a metalled road.

At the Youth Hostel, keep straight on along the signposted path for the Reserve. This leads to a tunnel under the A9. Beyond this, the paths through the fine woodland are well signposted.

The shorter walks are loops through the woodland and around two small lochans – the shortest of all is an all-abilities trail. The longest route is a lineal climb which leads out of the woodland and on to the open moor. Climb as far as the top of Craigellachie (overlooking Lochan Dubh), enjoy the views of the Cairngorms, then return by the same route.

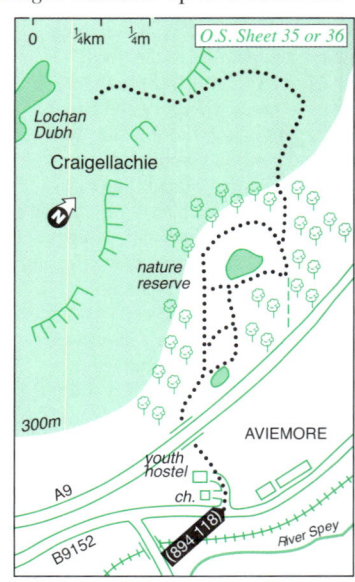